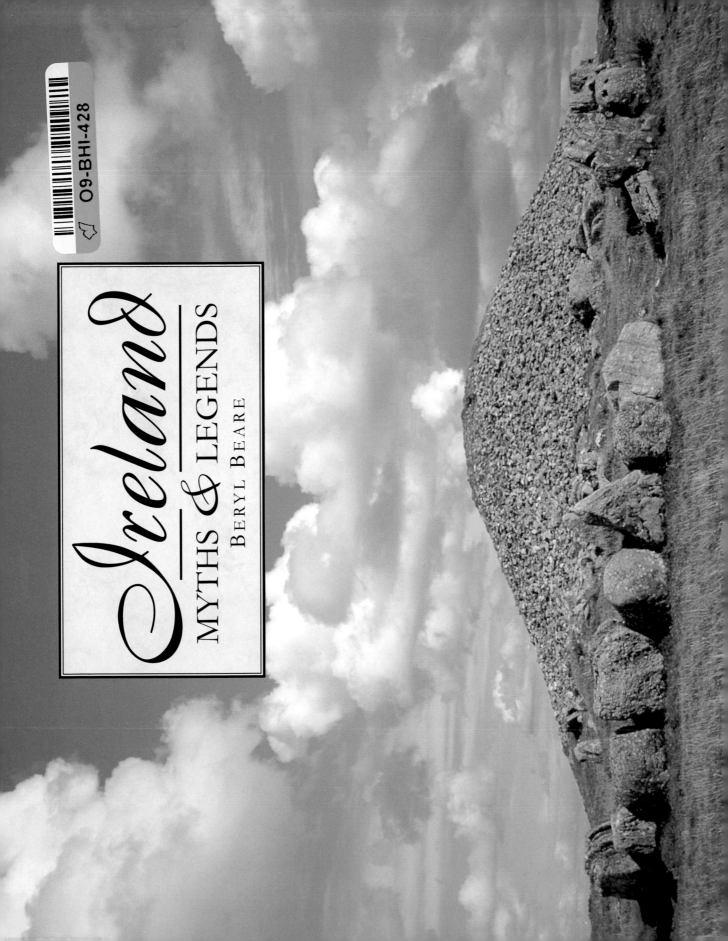

Ireland
MYTHS & LEGENDS

BERYL BEARE

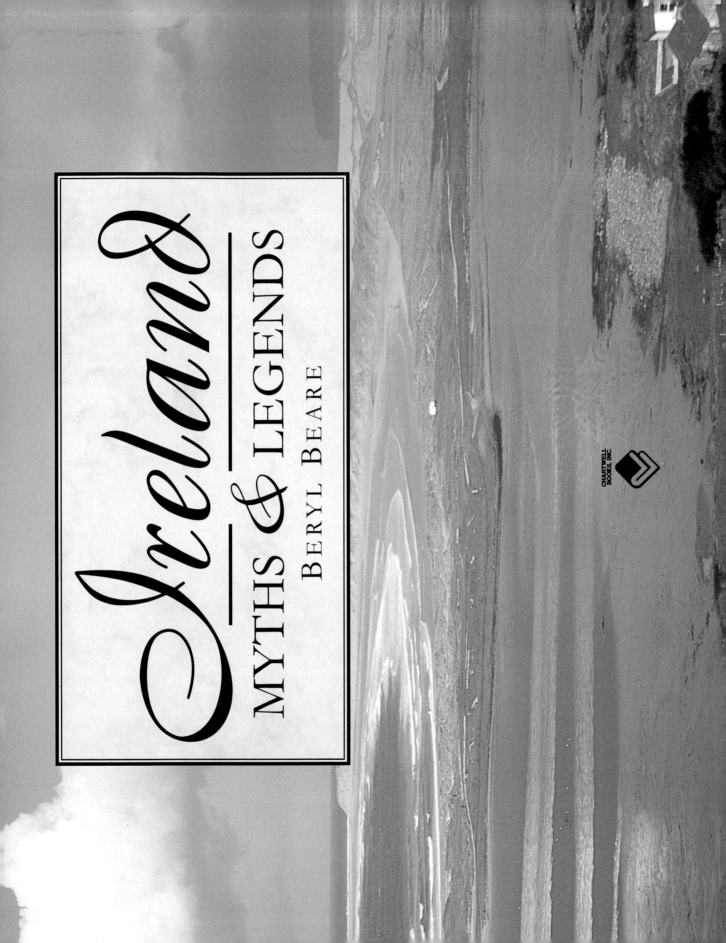

Ireland
MYTHS & LEGENDS

BERYL BEARE

CHARTWELL
BOOKS, INC.

Published by Chartwell Books
a division of Book Sales, Inc.
114 Northfield Avenue
Edison, NJ 08837

This edition produced for sale in the U.S.A.,
its territories and dependencies only.

First published in Great Britain in 1996 by
Parragon Books Limited
Units 13-17, Avonbridge Industrial Estate
Atlantic Road, Avonmouth, Bristol BS11 9QD
United Kingdom

Designed and produced by Touchstone
Old Chapel Studio, Plain Road, Marden
Tonbridge, Kent TN12 9LS United Kingdom

ISBN 0-7858-0538-9

Printed in Italy

Photographic credits:

(*Abbreviations: r = right, l = left, t = top, b = below*)

Images Colour Library: pages 1, 2-3, 5, 6-7, 8, 9, 10, 10-11, 12-13, 14-15, 16-17, 19, 20, 21, 22, 23, 27, 30-31, 32, 33, 34, 34-35, 36*t*, 37, 38, 39, 40, 41, 42-43, 44*t*, 44*b*, 45, 46, 50-51, 52, 53, 54, 55, 56, 57, 58, 59*t*, 59*b*, 60*t*, 60-61, 61*r*, 62-63, 64, 65, 66, 67*t*, 67*b*, 68*t*, 68*r*, 69, 70, 72-73, 74, 75, 76-77, 78, 79.

The Image Bank: pages 36*b*, 42*b*, 49*l*, 49*r*, 51*r*, 77*t*, 77*b*.

Greg Evans International: pages 24, 25, 29, 48*b*, 71.

Telegraph Colour Library: pages 28, 42*t*, 47, 48*t*.

Touchstone: page 18.

Colorific!: page 26.

The author would like to thank:

Rosemary Evans of the Northern Ireland
Tourist Board, Belfast.

The Navan Centre at Amagh for *Legends from the
North* (Cú Chulainn pages 8-15).

Fiona Campbell of Moyle District Council,
Ballycastle, and *The Nine Glens* by
Maureen Donnerly for *Legends from the North*
(pages 18-25) and *Fairies & Enchantments*
(pages 26-31).

The High Deeds of Finn MacCool by
Rosemary Sutcliffe for *Legends of Finn MacCool*
(pages 70-79).

Bord Fáilte – Irish Tourist Board, Dublin.

Right: The dramatic scenery of Conor Pass on the Dingle Peninsular, County Kerry.

Contents

Introduction

WONDERFUL, wistful – and sometimes weird, the myths and legends of Ireland have a fascination of their own. Many of the early myths were written down by Irish Christian scribes, just as they heard them from the *filids* – the Irish storytellers. In fact, some of the first Irish converts to Christianity may well have been *filids*.

Two great heroes emerge from Irish mythology, Cú Chulainn and Finn MacCool. Cú Chulainn (of the north), with his Red Branch Knights, is to Ireland what Arthur is to England and Wales. The epic tale of his stand against impossible odds, in defense of his country, continues to inspire the Irish people today. There is a statue of Cú Chulainn in the General Post Office in Dublin.

Finn MacCool belongs to a later date, and most of the stories are set in the softer countryside of the south. Finn's legends are not epic, but born of folklore and fairytale.

Fairies themselves – usually known as the Faery People, or the Little People – are, of course, prolific in Ireland. Their habits do not conform to the habits of other fairies, for rather than choosing to live at the bottom of a garden, they will often make their dwelling just outside a back door.

They have their Fairy Hills, as other fairies do, and they can be dangerous if upset. Nevertheless, they do not seem adverse to a little consideration from human householders.

Ireland is full of enchantment, and you will encounter many strange spells and charms along the way. It is doubtful whether you will meet the extraordinary charm known as the 'Blink' in any other country. And beware of Fairy Thorns – if you find one, whatever you do, DON'T dig it up!

There are monsters and beasties aplenty. Be warned, you could find some of them a little frightening. But one creature you are unlikely to meet is a dragon, unless – like the Dragon of Navan – it has been imported from overseas. This is because St Patrick successfully drove all the serpents out of Ireland, and serpents and dragons are closely related.

However, there are giants enough to make up for the missing dragons. Finn MacCool was sometimes portrayed as a giant, and the creation of the Giant's Causeway was attributed to him. In fact, the stone columns of this natural wonder look so perfect, that during World War II they were shelled by a German U-boat commander in mistake for British coastal fortifications!

Right: A land rich with myths and legends. The mysterious Piper Stones, County Wicklow.

IRELAND – MYTHS AND LEGENDS

Legends from the North

The Curse of Macha

Ulster

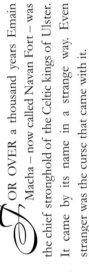

FOR OVER a thousand years Emain Macha – now called Navan Fort – was the chief stronghold of the Celtic kings of Ulster. It came by its name in a strange way. Even stranger was the curse that came with it.

A chieftain named Crunniac lived alone in the mountains, and one morning, after a terrible storm, he saw a woman running towards his house. She was very beautiful, but it was her extraordinary speed that astounded him. She moved across the rocky ground faster than any creature he had ever seen.

He invited her into the house, where she made herself at home at once. Then he asked her name, but on this point she refused to answer. Nevertheless, they fell in love and married, and doubtless Crunniac found terms of endearment to call her by. She proved an excellent wife, and their happiness was complete when she announced that she was pregnant.

One day they received a message from Conor, the King of Ulster. He invited them to a feast at the palace, with a fair and royal games in the grounds to follow.

Crunniac felt his wife should stay at home, the time for the baby's birth being so near. But the king had summoned them both, and so she accompanied him.

After a splendid feast the fair took place. There was music and dancing and much merriment, and the wine flowed freely. Finally, the moment came that everyone had been waiting for – the start of the chariot racing.

The king's horses were by far the fastest and won the races with ease. The crowd applauded loyally, declaring that nothing could beat them.

'My wife is faster,' said Crunniac rashly, having drunk too much wine. Angrily, the king called for Crunniac's wife and demanded that she should race against his horses.

'Not now!' she pleaded. 'Wait, please, until my child is born.' But the king told her Crunniac would be put to death if she refused. So she raced the king's chariot – and won.

'What is your name?' the king asked, astonished.

'My name is Macha,' she replied. Then, as the sky darkened and thunder rolled, she gave birth to twins – a boy and a girl.

'My twins will bring upon the men of Ulster a blessing and a curse!' she cried. 'The blessing will bring them power. The curse will make them weak when they most need strength.'

From that day the place was called Emain Macha – 'Twins of Macha' – and a curse was put on the men of Ulster.

Above: Remains of High Cross, County Donegal.
Left: The Mussenden Temple, County Derry.

The Hound of Cullan

Ulster

KING CONOR of Emain Macha had a little nephew called Setanta. The boy had not been born in Ulster, which meant that he was free of the curse of Macha that made men of Ulster weak when they most needed to be strong.

At the age of seven, Setanta left his home at Dundalk to join the Red Branch Knights at Emain Macha, who were famous for their skills of warfare. Setanta was the smallest boy in the troop, but none could out-run or out-smart him.

One night, the king attended a feast held by Cullan the blacksmith – a man who held the knowledge and the magic of turning cold iron into gleaming swords. Setanta begged to be allowed to finish a game with his friend, Ferdia, and promised to join his uncle later at Cullan's house.

By the time he had finished the game, night was falling. The journey was difficult, even by daylight, and it took Setanta much longer than he had expected.

Meanwhile, Cullan and his guests were having a splendid feast. Music was playing, wine was flowing – and no one remembered the little boy who would be arriving later.

Cullan's servants closed up his house for the night and let loose his favourite hound. This was the best guard dog Cullan had ever possessed; its strength and speed were unequalled, and it had teeth like daggers.

Setanta had no idea of the danger awaiting him as he struggled on towards Cullan's house. He arrived to find the gate closed, but being a good climber he was undeterred. As he started to climb, Cullan's hound sprang at him, knocking him to the ground.

Setanta leapt to his feet and felt the frenzy of battle rise within him – his muscles swelled and he grew visibly. Seizing the hound by the throat he lifted it high and dashed it against the wall, killing it instantly.

The servants, hearing the commotion and remembering Setanta, rushed out expecting to find him torn to pieces. There was great relief when he was found alive. But Cullan was angry at losing his loyal hound. So Setanta offered to act as a guard dog to him for one year, until a replacement could be found.

Cullan accepted the offer and gave the boy a new name – Cú Chulainn, which means 'the Hound of Cullan'.

Far Left: The beautiful Silent Valley and the Mountains of Mourne, County Down.
Left: The Silent Valley and Ben Crom, County Down.

— 11 —

The Cattle Raid of Cooley

Ulster

MAEVE WAS the Queen of Connacht and very jealous. She had as many jewels and warriors as her husband, King Ailill, but he had one possession she envied beyond words – he owned the White Bull of Connacht.

The queen heard that there was a great brown bull in Cooley, belonging to a man called Daire. To own this bull would make Maeve as rich in possessions as her husband, so she commanded her army to capture the Brown Bull of Cooley. They duly set off for Ulster, and their march was known as the Táin – the 'Cattle Raid'.

The warriors of Ulster were feverish and feeble, suffering from the curse of Macha that brought them weakness when they most needed strength. Only Cú Chulainn stood at a place called the 'Gap of the North', guarding the borders of Ulster against Maeve's armies.

Cú Chulainn, not born an Ulsterman, was the only warrior in the province to be spared the curse of Macha. Maeve's warriors had heard of him and trembled. Known as the Forge-Hound, or the Hound of Ulster, young Cú Chulainn was said to change into divine form when he engaged in battle.

The men from Connacht now witnessed the truth of this story. Cú Chulainn fought with the power of 20 men, slaying Maeve's warriors to right and left.

Eventually the cunning Maeve managed to bribe Cú Chulainn's great friend, Ferdia, to fight against him. Cú Chulainn was dismayed at the prospect of doing battle with his friend, but in the call of duty he had no choice.

Ferdia was himself a champion and the duel lasted for four days. On the fourth day Ferdia allowed Cú Chulainn the choice of weapons. The young warrior chose to fight with his personal weapon, the *gae bolga*, a spear with five points.

Ferdia was slain at last and, heavy hearted, Cú Chulainn praised his friend's courage as he died.

As suddenly as it had come, the curse of Macha was lifted and the warriors of Ulster joined Cú Chulainn to drive back Maeve's army. But the defeated Connacht men had already managed to capture the Brown Bull, and they drove it before them as they fled from their enemies.

At Connacht, the Brown Bull gored the White Bull to pieces, and then started on a wild rampage back to Cooley. But when he reached the place now called Druim Tarb – 'the Ridge of the Bull' – his heart burst and he dropped dead.

After all the bloodshed and misery, Queen Maeve had succeeded only in matching her husband's loss!

Left: The impressive sight of the Mourne Wall across the crest of the Mourne Mountains, County Down.

The Dragon of Navan

County Armagh

A RICH AND famous king of Ulster once heard of a plot to rob him of all his jewels. He locked them away quickly and called upon his wise men to advise him. The wise men, while looking wise, were singularly lacking in ideas and the king became very angry.

Suddenly, he heard the most beautiful and calming pipe music coming from outside the palace – and immediately sent a servant to fetch the piper.

The musician was brought before the king and bowed. He was hardly bigger than a fairy, dressed in many colours, with a peacock feather in his cap and a splendid set of pipes in his hand. He said that he had come to Armagh because he had heard of the king's troubles, and believed he could help.

'Your Majesty, I think the solution may be in China.'

The king said he had never heard of China.

'The land of dragons, Your Majesty.'

The king had no idea what a dragon was. So the musician explained that it would look fierce and watch over the king's jewels – and that he would be the only king in all Ireland to have a guard dragon.

The king had a boat made ready to take the musician to China to beg a dragon from the emperor. Eventually, the musician returned with a beautiful, fierce dragon in a huge cage. But as soon as the dragon was released it made straight for the lake behind the palace, jumped in – and disappeared.

The king was most upset, but the musician said this was exactly where he wanted the dragon to be.

'It will only come out of the lake when it hears my pipes. We will tie the jewels round the dragon's neck, and when Your Majesty wants them I will pipe the dragon out of the lake. At all other times it will remain at the bottom of the lake – where Your Majesty's jewels will be perfectly safe.'

This plan worked admirably until the piper – who was older than he looked – suddenly died. He was dozing by the water when he slipped off the stone he was sitting on and sank to the bottom of the lake, taking the pipes with him.

No other piper could bring the dragon out of the lake, and there he remains with the jewels. The king named the lake Loughnashade – 'the lake of the jewels'.

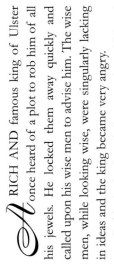

Left: Could this be the lake where the dragon still guards the jewels?

Finn and the Scottish Giant

The Giant's Causeway

FINN Mac CUMHAIL – or MacCool – is another famous hero of Ireland. You will be hearing more of him in the south, but here in Antrim he has a place, too. He is the legendary creator of the Giant's Causeway.

One day, it came to Finn's ears that a Scottish giant was ridiculing his fighting ability. Finn, the leader of fighters, was angered by this. He wrapped a challenge round a rock and threw it across the Irish Sea to Scotland.

Now the Scottish giant was not particularly brave. So he quickly sent a message back to Finn, saying that he would like to accept the challenge but could not do so because he was unable to swim across the sea.

Finn, however, was not prepared to let the challenge go this easily. He took his sword and hacked away at the great chunks of volcanic rock that littered the coast, making them into pillars. These he stood upright in the sea side by side, to form a causeway from Scotland to Ireland.

This left the giant no option but to accept the challenge. Which he did, albeit reluctantly.

When the giant arrived at Finn's house, the hero was nowhere to be seen. Finn's beautiful wife, Sava, invited him inside, explaining that Finn was away and only she and the baby were at home. Perhaps, she suggested, he would be kind enough to rock the baby while she prepared some refreshments.

The giant looked into the baby's cradle and was horrified. It must have been at least 18 feet (5.5m) long. If this was Finn's baby, how big was Finn going to be?

At that moment, the baby seized the giant's hand, stuck one of the fingers in its mouth – and bit it off. The giant gave a howl of pain and rushed from the house and back across the causeway. He never pointed the finger of scorn at Finn again!

Finn – who had been disguised as the baby – leapt from the cradle and ran in pursuit of the giant. He tore huge clods of earth from the land and hurled them after him.

One of the biggest holes he created filled with water and became Lough Neagh – the largest lake in Ireland.

The clod of earth missed the giant and fell into the Irish Sea, where it became what is known as the Isle of Man.

Right: Legend suggests that the amazing Giant's Causeway, County Antrim, was created by Finn MacCool.

LEGENDS FROM THE NORTH

Ballygalley Bay

County Antrim

THE COAST road from Larne to Cushendall leads to the Nine Glens of Antrim. Ballygalley is on this route, and looks out to the two lighthouses known as The Maidens.

Many years ago, a boat containing a dead woman and a baby girl drifted into Ballygalley Bay. No one knew from where these two had come, but the baby was still alive, and a coast-guard took her home and called her Marina Jane.

She grew into a beautiful young woman and married a sailor, who also owned a farm. He worked as both farmer and sailor for a number of years, and they lived very contentedly.

Then, one night when her husband was away on a sea voyage, Jane had a dream that he would never return.

Every day after that she went down to the beach to watch for his boat. The farm became neglected and – as her dream had foretold – he never returned. Eventually, the bailiffs arrived and Jane was forced to leave her cottage.

With her own hands she built a hut on the beach to live in, and gathered limpets for food. Her faithful dog, Brinie, seldom left her side – and even gave birth to four pups in the little hut.

One night there was a terrible storm and the sea rose threateningly. A neighbour offered Jane shelter, but she would not leave the hut in case her husband should return.

Brinie tried to pull her from the hut by her dress, but Jane refused to move.

However, the dog did manage to carry her four pups to safety.

The next morning the storm had abated, but on the beach there was no sign of Jane or her hut. It seemed that she had returned to the sea, from whence she had come.

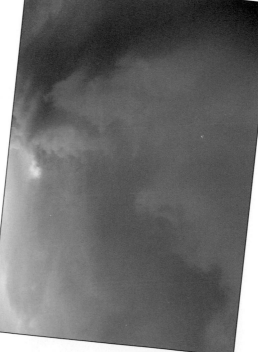

Above: Clouds gather over the coast as a storm moves in from the sea.

Right: The sea rises threateningly at sunset on the County Antrim coast.

The Banshee

Traditional

THE BANSHEE is an eerie spirit that is said to foretell death. Long ago, in Ireland, there lived a people called the Sidhe, who were feared for their magical powers. The women of this tribe – bansidhe, or 'women of the Sidhe' – with their unearthly wailing gave their name to the Banshee.

In all parts of Ireland it was the custom to 'wake' the dead – or to have a 'wake'. The corpse was then taken to the churchyard by a round-about route, as it was believed that the spirit of the deceased hovered near, and might return to the house if not sufficiently disorientated.

The Blink

The Glens

THE GLENSFOLK have always been superstitious, and in the old days they feared a particular spell known as the 'blink'. It was often associated with cattle, and cow's milk could be 'blinked' so that it would not churn to butter until the spell was charmed away.

Some people, however, could put the blink on anything, and one such person was known as 'Oul Ranal'.

There was a certain mare that, for reasons of his own, Ranal couldn't stand the sight of. One day he saw it being led down the road by its owner – and put the blink on it. The mare dropped dead instantly.

'Ah, hell to your soul, Ranal!' cried the owner, 'you've blinked me mare!'

Then he heaped such dire threats on to Ranal that the old man was forced to take the blink off again. No sooner had he done so than the mare got up, gave the harness a good shake, and trotted off as lively as ever.

Red yarn was said to keep the blink away, and was often seen on the horns of cows and goats. But it had other uses, too.

A farmer was shooting rabbits in the mountains one day, when he caught his foot in a rabbit hole and twisted his ankle.

With great difficulty he managed to hobble down to the inn – thinking that a rest and a few drinks might serve as a cure. But the ankle swelled up so much that it broke the very laces on his boot.

The winter beauty of County Antrim as snow settles on The Giant's Causeway, above, and Cushendall and Red Bay, right.

He was taken home in a great deal of pain, and his wife applied cold compresses to the injury. But they had no effect, and the pain was as bad as ever. So she helped him on to his horse and sent him to see Katie McGreer.

Katie was known for her ability with charms, and was particularly good at taking off the blink.

This was no blink, however, but a very painful sprain. She chanted a few words and then tied a red yarn round the farmer's swollen ankle.

By the time he arrived home again he was able to leap off his horse, his ankle looked normal – and he was no longer in pain.

Red yarn, it seems, was good to have around!

Deidre of the Sorrows

Ulster

A HARPIST TO King Conchubar of Ulster had a baby daughter named Deidre. When the child uttered her first cry, a Druid made the prophecy that she would be the most beautiful girl in Ireland – and that her beauty would bring trouble and sorrow to many.

To avoid such sorrow, Deidre's father sent her away to be brought up by a foster mother in a remote forest hut. In this lonely place the girl had no contact with the outside world at all. But one night, when she was about 15 years old, a hunter arrived at the hut. He had become lost in the forest and was seeking hospitality. Reluctantly, the foster mother admitted him. When the hunter saw Deidre he was amazed by her beauty, and decided she would make a fitting wife for the king.

On his return to Emain Macha he told King Conchubar of the girl's beauty, and explained where she could be found. The king visited the hut and saw Deidre for himself. He fell in love with her and wanted to marry her at once. She, however, pleaded for a year in which to prepare herself for her royal duties.

That winter, three of the noblest young men in Ireland passed through the forest. They were brothers – the Sons of Usnach – and Deidre fell in love with the tallest and bravest of the three. His name was Naoise, and he returned her love – although both knew it must bring sorrow, for she was promised to the king.

Naoise and Deidre, accompanied by Naoise's two brothers, fled to Scotland. When King Conchubar heard of this he was furious and sent for the usurped ruler of Ulster, Fergus Mac Roigh, to bring them back.

The king promised that no harm would befall them. Fergus accepted his word and set off

Below: The mysterious Beaghmore stone circles, Co. Tyrone.

Right: The Celtic remains of Ossian's Grave, Co. Antrim.

for Scotland. He was trusted by Naoise and his brothers, so the three warriors and Deidre returned to Emain Macha.

King Conchubar, however, had no intention of keeping the promise he had made to Fergus. As soon as they landed in Ireland – on the flat rock now known as the 'Rock of Usnach' – he sent his warriors to kill the three brothers.

When Naoise was slain, Deidre could not bear to go on living and took her own life. To this day she is remembered as 'Deidre of the Sorrows'.

The Dance of Death

Fair Head

ABOVE THE Rock of Usnach is the great headland called Fair Head. It was the sad fate of a beautiful, golden-haired girl that gave the headland its name.

She lived in a castle on Rathlin Island, and had many suitors. Among them were two particularly ardent young men who decided to fight for her hand. It was agreed that the winner would marry her.

One of the young men was fatally wounded, and his loyal servant, Thol Dhu, hurried to his side. As the young man lay dying, he whispered to the servant to dance with the girl out on the cliff below the castle.

Thol Dhu whirled her into a giddy dance that took them to the very edge of the cliff. Before the girl realized what was happening, he had danced with her right over the edge and into the sea.

Both were drowned – Thol Dhu having sacrificed his own life to avenge his young master. The girl's body was washed ashore on the mainland, and because of her lovely golden hair the spot came to be known as 'Fair Head'.

Right: The ruins of Dunluce Castle, County Antrim.

The Stranger from the Lough

County Antrim

THERE WAS once an old woman called Mary McAnulty who made her living by gathering dulse (seaweed) below Fair Head. Because she always used the entrance to the Grey Man's Path on the headland, it came to be known as 'Mary McAnulty's Hall Door'.

One evening at dusk, as she was returning home with a bag of dulse on her back, she met a fine gentleman near her 'hall door'. He walked with her to the banks of Lough Dhu, where, as usual, she sat down to rest.

She then noticed that his hair was green, and remarked upon the fact. He explained that it was probably because he had lived for years beneath the waters of the lough.

They walked on for a bit and then sat down to rest again. This time, the gentleman put his head on Mary's lap and went to sleep. But while he slept she noticed his cloven hoof, and slipped away as quickly as she could.

When the fine stranger awoke and found her gone, he immediately changed into a devil-horse. He gave a terrifying neigh that could be heard for miles, and then returned to his dwelling in Lough Dhu. He is probably still there today!

Above: Carrick-A-Rede rope bridge, County Antrim.

Fairies & Enchantments

Fairies

Traditional Folk Tale

FAIRIES ARE so numerous in Ireland that some people believe all fairies are Irish! Folk memory of 'strange wee men' may well have originated from the neolithic men in Ireland called 'Firbolgs', who were said to have hidden from their enemies in holes and underground dwellings. An old word for the men of the hillocks is 'Fearsihe' – pronounced 'Faery'.

Whatever their origin, fairies are generally respected by the glensfolk, and not without good reason. It is considered very unwise to offend a fairy – and most unlucky to interfere with fairy property. Those who have tried to remove, or cut down, a Fairy Thorn will vouch for this.

Right: Ruins of ancient villages can be seen all over Ireland – could this be where the Fairy folk live?

man, which grows on its own or on some ancient cairn or 'rath' (fort). There are some very strange stories told of these fairy bushes.

A farmer's son wanted to build a little hut for his rabbits. He chose a site in one of his father's fields and started to dig, not realizing he was near a Fairy Thorn. Suddenly, he heard a voice saying, 'Don't dig here!'

Fairy Thorns

Traditional Folk Tale

A FAIRY THORN or 'skeogh', is described as being one not planted by

He paused for a moment, then thought he must have been hearing things and started to dig again. Once more he heard a voice saying 'Don't dig here!'

This time he felt sure a friend was playing a trick on him, so he searched about – but could find no sign of a living soul. Puzzled, he started to dig again, and at once the voice became loud and angry: 'DON'T DIG HERE!'

He didn't stay to argue. He headed quickly for home with his spade – and decided to find a different site for his rabbit hut!

Another man, a farmer of Glendun, wanted to remove a Fairy Thorn that was growing on his farm. So he took his axe and hacked away at it.

After a blow or two the blade 'turned' on him and almost gashed his leg. So he fetched another axe, but as soon as he started to cut at the Fairy Thorn, blood began to ooze out of the stem. That was too much for him. He gave up and went home to his bed. The next morning all his hair had fallen out, and he had to wear a wig for the rest of his days.

Right: The picturesque Mourne Mountains, Co. Down.

Hallowe'en

Traditional

THE IRISH name for Hallowe'en – or, in the glens, 'Halloweve' – is 'Samhain', the eve of All Saints. Part of the festivities were to celebrate the return of those who had been away all summer on high pastures with the cattle – 'booleying'.

It was also a night (31 October) when the living felt the presence of the dead, and strange things could happen. And it was the time for playing tricks on neighbours – even to the extent of removing doors and gates – and blaming the fairies!

Lammas Fair

County Antrim

LAMMAS FAIR, the feast of 'Lu', has an unbroken history of over 300 years. It marks the end of summer and the beginning of harvest and, in the old days, offerings of flowers and fruit were made at Holy Wells.

Held at Ballycastle, the fair offers a brisk trade in the sale of livestock. Also on sale are such delights as 'yellow man' (a hard yellow toffee) and 'dulse', the edible seaweed that is gathered locally. These are mentioned in a famous old song.

'At the Ould Lammas Fair, boys, were you
ever there,
At the Ould Lammas Fair in
Ballycastle, oh?
Did you treat your Mary Ann to Dulse
and 'yellow man',
At the Ould Lammas Fair at
Ballycastle, oh?'

Left: The ruins of Loughinisland Church, County Down and its ancient graveyard. Strange things could happen in the presence of the dead at Hallowe'en.

The Milk Charm

County Antrim

HERE WAS once an old woman who had a strange magical power. She could draw milk to herself from the cows by murmuring an incantation, but only when the moon was right for it.

One bright moonlit night, a man wearing a large pair of knee boots was riding his horse along the road to Cushendall. Suddenly, ahead of him, he saw an old woman standing on a grassy hillock with her arms stretched out in front of her.

'Come a' to me,' she was saying. 'Come a' to me.' The man didn't know the old woman, but he reined in his horse to see what she was doing.

He knew it was some kind of spell, and he didn't believe in that sort of thing himself. However, he thought he would have a joke with the old woman.

He threw up his own arms, straight and stiff in front of him.

'Come some to me,' he said loudly. 'Come some to me!'

Instantly, his knee boots were filled with milk. He spurred his horse to a gallop and stopped only when he was safely home.

Left: The shore from Lough Eske, on the route of the Ulster Way, is typical of the beauty of County Donegal.

The Swan Children

Ulster

$\mathcal{L}$ONG AGO, a chieftain named Lir had four children: a daughter called Fionnuala, a son called Aodh, and twin boys called Fiachra and Conn.

His wife died following the birth of the twins and, for the sake of the children, Lir agreed to marry her sister, Aoife. For a time all went well and Aoife honoured her sister's children. But then she became very jealous and decided to get rid of them.

Now, Aoife had the power of witchcraft. So she took the children to Lough Dairbhreach – the 'Lake of the Oaks' – and turned them into four beautiful swans.

The spell was to last for 900 years, 300 of which the swans would spend on Lough Dairbhreach, 300 on the Sruth na Maoile, in the Irish Sea, and 300 years on the island called Inis Gluaire. Their stepmother allowed them to keep their mortal voices – and to sing the sweetest music in the world.

Lir went in search of his children and found them on Lough Dairbhreach. Fionnuala explained what had happened and he was heartbroken. But people came from far and wide to hear the beauty of their singing, and so they lived out their 300 years of enchantment on the lough.

The sea around Sruth na Maoile, where they spent the next 300 years, was rough and wild. The

great waves often swept them apart, but they always agreed to meet on Carraig na Ron – the 'Rock of the Seals'.

After 300 years they went to Inis Gluaire. Christianity had now come to the island and St Mochaomhog lived there. One day, he saw the four swans swimming on a lake and asked if they were the children of Lir. They replied that they were, and he offered them holy sanctuary.

Deoch, wife of the King of Connacht, had heard of the swans and wanted them to entertain her. The king went to fetch them, but the holy man refused to give them up.

Angrily, the king seized them from the altar. As soon as he touched them the spell was broken, and they turned into three withered old men and one withered old woman.

The king fled in terror, and Fionnuala asked the holy man to baptize them, as they were near death. They were then buried together and a stone was set over them with their names upon it.

Left: The coastline of Ulster can be rough and wild or calm and beautiful. Here we see the wide stretches of sand of County Donegal.

Tales from Connacht

The Crowing Cock

County Galway

THERE WAS once a man in Galway who was working in a field near his house. Whenever he looked towards his house, he saw a coffin descending from the sky. At the moment the coffin came down the March cock, inside the house, would shake his wings and crow loudly. And he would keep crowing until the coffin disappeared.

This went on for about three weeks, and each day the man saw the coffin descending until the cock crowed and banished it. But the man's wife came to hate the cock because of the noise it made.

One day, the man saw the coffin coming down on the side of the house. But he didn't hear the cock crow, and the coffin stayed where it was. Troubled, he went into the house – and there he found the cock dead.

His wife said she had thrown a mallet at the bird to drive it away, because her head was splitting from its crowing. But the mallet hit the cock on the head, and killed it.

'Then you have killed me, too!' cried her husband.

Sure enough he was right, for two days later he was dead.

The Fisherman's Strange Catch

County Galway

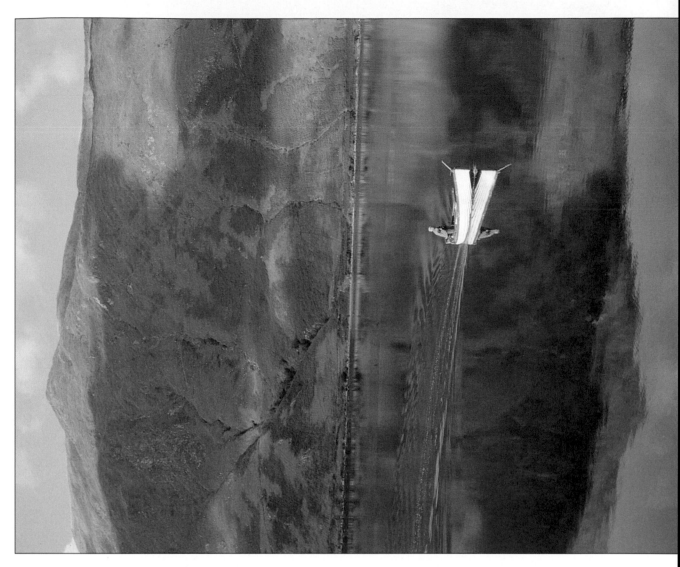

A FISHERMAN from Errismore once landed an unexpected catch. It was towards evening, the day had been fine and the fish plentiful. Suddenly, he felt a great weight on his line, and thought he had hooked a particularly large fish.

He hauled it in and saw, to his amazement, that he had caught a small boy with red hair. The fisherman had always wanted a son, so he was very pleased with his catch.

He took the boy home, but as soon as he put him down on the floor, the child rushed under a bed. And there he stayed until the following day.

Even when the man succeeded in getting him out from under the bed, the boy would neither eat nor drink. The fisherman tried to tempt him with the most appetizing food he could find, and told him what a good life they would have together. But the boy just sat silently, looking unhappy.

The fisherman felt very sad, but he knew what he must do. He took the boy in his boat, to the place where he had caught him. The little lad gave one joyous laugh, dived down into the water like a cormorant – and was seen no more.

Left: Cottages on the Gorumna Islands, County Galway.
Right: Fishing in Connemara, County Galway.

The Giant Rat

County Galway

A POOR MAN in Galway had a wife and four children. One morning, as they sat down to breakfast, the largest rat any of them had ever seen came into the kitchen. It jumped up on to the table and ate the breakfast – and the family was much too frightened to stop it.

When the rat had finished eating it jumped off the table and went out. It returned when the man came home for his supper, jumped up on to the table as before, and ate the food.

'God help us!' cried the man. 'We shall starve to death.'

Above right: Traditional turf bog, Killary Harbour, County Galway.

Right: Inishnee Island, County Galway.

Next day he bought a cat that was known to be a good ratter. When the rat came in, it saw the cat sitting by the fire and sidled up to her. Then the fight began.

The cat just managed to escape with her life. The rat calmly jumped up on to the table and ate the food. When it had eaten its fill, it left the house as usual.

The cat licked her wounds by the fire and drank some milk. Then she, too, went out.

The cat stayed out all night, and when the man came home from work the following evening, she still hadn't returned.

'We're finished now,' he said. 'That thieving rat will kill us for sure!'

The rat came in to supper, ate the food and left. It kept coming back for three nights and three days, but there was no sign of the cat. On the fourth morning she returned – and with her was the biggest cat that anyone had ever seen.

The big cat sat by the hearth and the small cat sat on a chair.

'Bring in a quart of milk for the cats,' the man said to his wife.

The cats drank their milk and the man sat down to his breakfast – and, as usual, in came the rat. When it saw the big cat it paused. Then they both sprang at each other in the centre of the room.

They fought in the kitchen all morning, and they fought up and down the yard all afternoon. At sunset, the huge cat finally managed to kill the giant rat.

Both cats then drank their milk and left the house together – and neither was ever seen again.

Above: Beautiful lake scene in Connemara, County Galway.

Left: Dunguair Castle, County Galway proudly flies the flag.

The Bald Man of Bulben

County Sligo

FINN MacCOOL and his mighty army, the Fianna, were hunting deer on Ben Bulben, Finn's favourite mountain. They had an unusually bad day, however, and sat down to play dice in the evening feeling very hungry. While they were playing, a bald man approached them.

'Good evening, Bald Man,' said Finn.

'It is not good,' said the bald man, 'because my wife has left me.'

'That is bad, Bald Man,' said Finn.

'That is not bad,' said the bald man, 'because I have my children, and also twenty litters of pigs.'

'That is good, Bald Man,' said Finn.

'That is good,' agreed the bald man, 'because one of the litters is fat and ready to eat, and I invite you and your men to feast with me.'

Finn accepted the invitation gratefully, and asked the bald man where he lived.

'There are four ends to the world,' the bald man replied, 'and whichever one you choose, you shall arrive at my door.'

Finn and the Fianna set off. After much walking and even more heated discussion, they came to a wood. In the wood they saw a light, which they followed, and it led them to the bald man's house.

'You must be starving,' said the bald man, opening his door to them. Finn and the Fianna admitted that they were, indeed, very hungry.

'The pig litters are all sleeping,' said the bald man. 'You must kill the litter on which we shall feast without waking the old sow, or any of the piglets.'

The Fianna, with all their combat skills, considered this to be an easy task. But in fact none of them managed to kill the pigs, and the bald man had to kill them himself. The pigs were then prepared for the pot, cooked and served up at table.

'Truly, this is an excellent feast,' said Finn, appreciatively.

'That is good,' said the bald man, 'if you can keep it from those now coming in at the door.'

Instantly, the Fianna raised their eyes from the table to the door. When they cast their eyes back to the feast again, it had completely disappeared.

Once more, they found themselves on Ben Bulben playing dice, and feeling hungrier than ever. Realizing they had been tricked, they made their way wearily homeward – and resolved never again to accept an invitation from a bald man on Ben Bulben!

Left: The magnificent mountain Ben Bulben, County Sligo, boasts a great many myths and legends.

Brothers of the Fish Charm

County Sligo

LONG AGO, in the county of Sligo, lived a king and queen who had no children. The king asked his chief adviser what he should do, and the chief adviser – who happened to be one of the faery people – told him about the fish charm.

One of the king's servants must fish where Lough Gill, the bright lake, touched Dooney Rock, and bring home the seventh fish he caught. The fish must then be prepared for the queen's breakfast, and no blob or blister must appear on the skin.

The seventh fish was duly caught and prepared for the queen. However, while it was heating, a small blob appeared. The cook, making sure she was unobserved, hastily smoothed the blob and then quickly licked her finger.

The queen ate the fish with relish, except for the head and tail which were thrown into the yard and eaten by the mare and the greyhound.

Within the year, to the delight of the whole kingdom, the queen gave birth to a baby son. The cook, who had tasted the fish, also had a son – the mare had a foal and the greyhound had three pups!

It was customary in those days for children to be sent to foster parents, who cared for them until they grew up. So it was with Dara, the queen's son, and Conn, the cook's son. When they were eighteen years old, they both returned to the palace in Sligo.

They thought of themselves as true brothers, and they were so alike that no one could tell them apart. This did not please the queen, who was unwilling for the cook's son to enjoy the same privilege as the king's son.

She went to her husband's chief adviser, and he instructed a servant to put a mark on Dara's neck. The servant would know the queen's son, because as the two youths walked together through the palace door, the royal son would bow his head.

Dara did, indeed, bow his head – and the mark was made upon his neck. The queen then knew which young man must be sent away, and she dismissed Conn from the palace.

Dara gave Conn a horse for his journey and the two boys parted sadly. Conn waved farewell, and was carried along by the 'sidhe-gaoth' – the Faery Wind.

Far Left: Classiebawn Castle, Mullaghmore, County Sligo at sunset.
Right: The ruins of Ballingdon Abbey overlooks Lough Arrow, County Sligo.

Conn and the Giants

Connacht

THE FAERY WIND carried Conn to a distant palace, where the king employed him as a herdsman for his cows. But there were no pastures where the cows could graze, only a field full of stones.

Conn hunted about and eventually found a field with lush green grass. He drove the cows in and was congratulating himself on the discovery, when an angry giant appeared. The giant was the owner of the field.

'Fight, dwarf,' the giant commanded, 'or I'll grind you up to make snuff for my nose!'

Conn trembled, but he fought the giant just the same. The giant was huge and strong, but Conn was nimble and clever, and the fight lasted all day. At evening, Conn mustered all his strength and brought the giant to his knees.

'Spare me,' pleaded the giant, 'and I'll give you my best gift — the sword that nothing can stand against. Here, try it out on that tree-stump.'

Conn took the sword, but he didn't try it out on the tree-stump. Instead, he cut off the giant's head with one deft stroke. Then, as the head flew through the air, Conn cut it in two.

The following day, Conn returned with the cows to the same field. He had only been there a short time when another giant appeared. This giant had two heads and spoke with two mouths. He also commanded Conn to fight — and, again, Conn did so.

Once more, he summoned all his strength at evening and brought the two-headed giant to his knees. The giant pleaded for mercy with both his mouths and offered Conn his best gift — the cloak of invisibility.

Conn took the cloak and tried it on. Being invisible, it was not difficult to cut off both the giant's heads with a sweep of his sword. As the heads flew high in the air, Conn cut the two into four.

The next day, at the field, another giant appeared. This giant had four heads and, like the others, was brought to his knees at sunset. His gift was a pair of shoes that travelled faster than the wind. With a mighty sweep of his sword, Conn cut off the giant's four heads and then sliced the four into eight.

After that he decided to look for another field, for he didn't think he could handle an eight-headed giant!

Left: The mysterious standing stones near Blacksod Point, County Mayo.
Right: The lush green shores of Doo Lough, County Mayo.

Above: Fishing on Doo Lough, County Mayo.

Above: One of the many ancient towers that can still be seen in County Mayo.

Right: The island of Inisfree, Lough Gill, County Sligo.

The Enchanted Bridegrooms

County Sligo

THERE WAS once a man living in County Sligo called Fintan the Great. He had three beautiful daughters, who were courted by three worthy brothers – Ainle, Conan and Diarmuid.

Fintan was pleased with the three prospective bridegrooms, and arranged a great feast to celebrate the weddings. He gave to each of his daughters a generous dowry – to the eldest, her weight in gold; to the middle daughter, her weight in silver; and to the youngest, her weight in copper.

After the ceremonies and feasting, the three couples set off together. They bade farewell to Fintan, each promising to return in one year and one day.

At the end of one year, Fintan made great preparations to welcome his daughters and their husbands back to Sligo. But the final day passed, and there was no sign of them. Fintan waited for two more weeks, and then he sent his son, Ladra, to search for the young couples.

On the road, Ladra met a red-headed man who would not reveal his name, but who said he knew what had happened to Ainle, Conan and Diarmuid. They had been bewitched by the Giant of Fomor.

For some reason, the giant bore a grudge against the three brothers. He had turned Ainle into a ram, Conan into a salmon and Diarmuid into an eagle.

Ladra and the red-headed man decided to enlist the help of other rams, eagles and salmon. Word spread quickly through the animal kingdom, and help was offered.

A salmon said he had seen a mole under the giant's arm when he went fishing, and knew that was his vulnerable spot. A ram said he knew that if a turtle's egg should touch the giant's mole, then his power would be destroyed. An eagle said he would watch with his sharp eyes and tell them when the giant was going fishing.

So the plan was laid. When the giant next went fishing, the red-headed man aimed a turtle's egg at the vulnerable mole. His aim was excellent – and the giant fell dead.

The three enchanted brothers returned to their human form, and were reunited with their brides, who had been searching for them. The brothers greeted the red-headed man joyfully. He had concealed his identity out of fear – for he was the fourth brother and the giant had also born him a grudge!

The Fairy's Question

County Sligo

AT FUNERALS in County Sligo, the spade and the shovel are left in the shape of a cross at the open grave. This is a custom that has been handed down from St Patrick.

The saint had a servant called Domhnaill, and one day he was collecting wood to make a fire. He collected such a large bundle that he was unable to lift it by himself.

Suddenly, a small man – one of the Faery People – appeared, lifted the bundle and set it down where the fire was to be lit. Domhnaill thanked the little man, who declared that he must do him a favour in return.

'Tomorrow,' said the fairy, 'while St Patrick is saying the mass, ask him what will become of the Little People on the Last Day of Judgement.'

Domhnaill put the fairy's question to St Patrick in the middle of the church service. The saint, surprised at the interruption, replied, 'They will be lost.' Afterwards, he asked his servant why he had put the question to him at such a time.

Domhnaill explained that it had been the fairy's bargain, and that he must return next day with the reply.

'I know that the Faery People will not be pleased with the answer,' he said, unhappily.

St Patrick was concerned for his servant's safety. 'You must keep the bargain you have made with the fairy,' he said, 'but you must also protect

Above: Clew Bay viewed from Croagh Patrick.

Left: St. Patrick's statue overlooks County Mayo.

Right: Croagh Patrick at sunset.

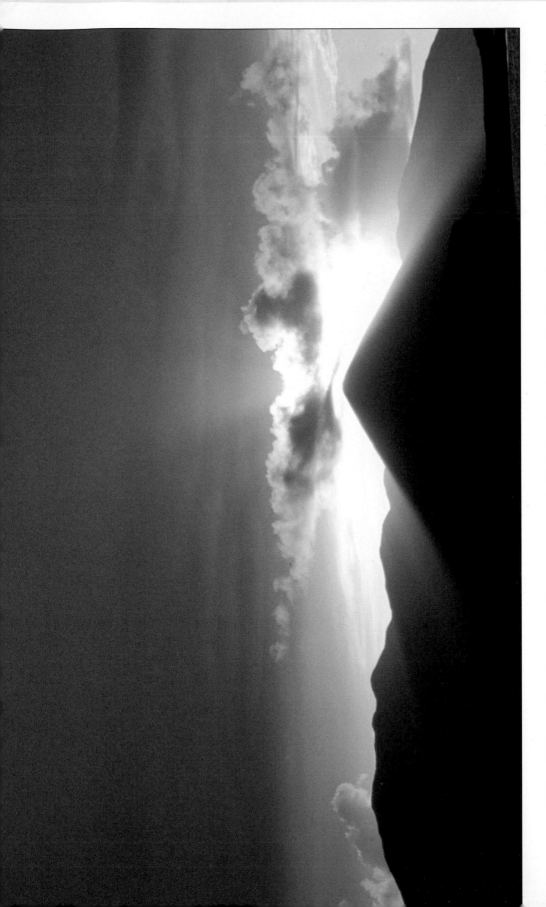

yourself.' He told Domhnaill to dig a grave wide and deep enough to lie in, and to stay in it for one whole day.

At the top of the grave, the spade and shovel must be placed in the form of a cross, to ward off evil spirits. The next day Domhnaill returned to the fairy, who asked the question: 'What will happen to the Little People on the Last Day?'

'They will be lost,' Domhnaill replied.

Immediately, the shrieks and screams of millions of fairies were heard. A terrible storm broke out, lightning flashed and thunder rolled as it had never rolled before.

The fairies were in a terrible, vengeful mood – but Domhnaill remained safe beneath his cross in the ground.

Eventually, the fairies' cries became a plaintive wailing. Domhnaill stayed in his grave for two days, and then emerged safely.

The crossed spade and shovel have been placed over newly dug graves ever since.

Hawk's Well

County Sligo

THE HAWK'S WELL at Tullaghnan, on the slopes of the Ox Mountains, is one of the wonders of Ireland. Its origin, like that of the crossed spade and shovel, is attributed to St Patrick.

The saint was on the peak of a mountain in County Mayo, which is now known as Croagh Patrick. There he banished all the serpents and demons out of Ireland and into the sea, where they drowned.

However, one demon-serpent managed to escape. This demon was known as Caorthannach, sometimes called the Fire-Spitter, and it was even said that she was the devil's mother.

The demon slid down the side of Ox Mountain thinking that she was unobserved. But St Patrick saw her, and was determined that no demon should remain in Ireland. At the foot of the mountain, the fastest horse in County Mayo was brought for him to ride. The saint mounted, and set off in pursuit of Caorthannach, the Fire-Spitter.

The demon sped northwards, spitting fire as she went. She knew that St Patrick would need water to quench his thirst, so she poisoned every well that she passed.

The saint became more and more thirsty as he pursued the demon. But he knew he must not drink from the contaminated wells, and rode on. When he reached Tullaghan, in County Sligo, he was so desperately thirsty that he prayed for a drink.

Far left: An impressive view of Achill Island on the Atlantic coast of County Mayo.

Suddenly, his horse stumbled on a rock and St Patrick was thrown to the ground. As he fell, his hand and back struck a stone – and where he landed, a well sprang up beside him.

The water from this well was fresh and safe to drink, and the saint drank from it until his thirst was quenched. Then he hid himself in a hollow beside Carraig-an-Seabhach – the Hawk's Rock – and waited for the Fire-Spitter.

Above: The tempestuous Bunderragha River with Delphi mountain in the background.

As the demon approached, St Patrick sprang out and banished her with one word. The Fire-Spitter drowned in the Atlantic Ocean, and the swell she created flowed into the well. It is now a healing well and ebbs and flows with the tide – containing first fresh, and then salt water.

The mark of St Patrick's hand and back, where he fell from his horse, and the imprint of the horse's hoof can still be seen on the stones by the well.

Above: Twelve Pins Mountain, Connemara.

Left: Connemara ponies, a breed for which Ireland is well known.

The Little People

Connacht

> 'Come away, O human child!
> To the waters and the wild
> With a faery, hand in hand . . .'
> W.B. Yeats

THE FAERY PEOPLE – or the Little People – frequently made their homes near the houses of humans. They usually lived close to the surface, beneath the ground. Irish women, when throwing dirty water out of the back door, would often call a warning to the fairies first.

At Hallowe'en and May Eve the fairies were particularly active, and babies and newly married brides were very vulnerable to their magic.

Mary was the new bride of Sean, and one May Eve she was watching her mother-in-law baking in the kitchen. The older woman asked Mary if she had hung out the whin (gorse) bushes to prevent the fairies from coming into the house. The girl replied that she had, but as soon as she had hung the prickly gorse on the wall, a strange child had appeared and taken it in her hands.

Suddenly, the same child appeared at the door, holding out an empty cup. Mary filled the cup with milk, and the child disappeared. Then a little old man appeared, and asked for a light for his pipe.

Mary carried a lighted coal to the door for the old man's pipe and then he, too, disappeared.

TALES FROM CONNACHT

Just then Sean, Mary's husband, came home, but he had seen neither the child nor the little old man.

Sean's mother felt the power of the Faery People, and was vexed that Mary should have offered milk and fire on May Eve. As Sean was giving Mary the ribbons he had brought home for her, another child came in by the door. This child was so mild-mannered and polite that even Sean's mother welcomed her warmly.

The child asked for a space to be cleared so that she may dance. As soon as the dance began, Mary was enchanted. Sean and his mother became alarmed, for this was obviously a faery child and had cast a spell on the household.

Sean tried to coax his young wife away from the child – but in vain. The faery magic was luring Mary away to the enticing charms of Fairyland.

For a moment she hesitated as she saw the love in her husband's face. But the moment was lost. Mary left, hand in hand with the faery child, and was never seen again. . .

Above and Left: The unspoilt and rugged countryside of Connemara, County Galway.

The Mermaid of Sligo

County Sligo

A CHIEFTAIN of Tireragh, west of the bay of Sligo, once fell in love with a beautiful mermaid. She was sitting on a rock combing her long golden hair when he first saw her. After that, he went down to the shore every day to look for her – and each day he fell more in love.

One morning, to his great delight, he saw that she was sleeping beneath her magic mantle. If a mermaid loses her magic mantle she also loses her 'fish body', and while still longing for the sea, assumes the character and appearance of a mortal woman.

Very quietly, the chieftain crept up on the mermaid, removed the magic mantle – and hid it among the rocks.

The mermaid awoke without her fish tail and saw the chieftain. She immediately fell in love with him and he, overjoyed, carried her away from the seashore to become his bride.

They lived together happily, and had seven children. The chieftain always kept the magic mantle well hidden – for he knew that if the mermaid saw it, the lure of the sea would be too great for her.

One day, when the youngest boy was about four years old, the chieftain decided to move the magic mantle to a more secure hiding place. The little boy watched as his father carried the mantle, and could not take his eyes off it. It seemed to

contain every shade and colour of the sea, and at the same time it flashed and glittered like the sunlight on top of the waves.

He ran to tell his mother of his exciting new discovery. But she appeared not to share his delight, and didn't laugh in her usual way.

Instead, she became very solemn and asked him to take her to the place where the mantle was hidden. As soon as she set eyes on her mantle, she was filled with an overwhelming longing for the sea. She took her seven children down to the seashore with her and then touched them, one by one, with the magic mantle.

As they were touched, the children turned to stone – and seven stones then stood forlornly upon the shore. The mermaid regained her fish body and disappeared into the ocean, and was never seen again.

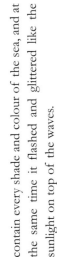

Left: The dramatic Atlantic coastline of Ireland is the setting for a number of myths and legends.

Above: There are many standing stones in Ireland, this stone circle is found at Ardgroom, County Cork.

The Monster of Lake Glenade

County Sligo

LAKE MONSTERS have different names in different countries. Scotland has its water-kelpies (even the Loch Ness Monster could be a water-kelpie in another form), Wales has its afancs, and England its 'worms', or dragons.

They all have one thing in common, however – they are wickedly fierce and do not make good pets. The Irish lake monster is no exception. It is called the Dabharchú, or 'Hound of the Deep', and is possibly the fiercest of all.

Many years ago, a young bride was washing clothes on the edge of Lake Glenade. She was surprised to see how much of a splash she was making – then the splashing increased and the hideous Dabharchú appeared. She had time to give one terrified scream before it devoured her.

Her husband, Terence, was hunting in the woods nearby when he heard the scream. Immediately, he rushed to the lake – gun in hand.

There he saw the clothes floating on the water, but no sign of his bride. Suddenly, there was a great splashing and the frightful Dabharchú rose from the lake once again. Taking careful aim, Terence shot it dead.

As the lifeless body of the Dabharchú fell back into the water, there was a shriek-like roar from the lake – so loud that it drew people from miles around. An old man explained that there were two Dabharchús in the lake – a loving pair – and the living one was now mourning the death of its mate.

'Either you or the Dabharchú must die,' the old man told Terence. 'My advice to you is to get as far away from the lake as possible.'

Terence saddled his horse and rode as fast as he could for Ben Bulben. He was hotly pursued by the Dabharchú's furious companion, which moved almost as fast on land as it did in the water.

Terence arrived on the other side of Ben Bulben, at Cashelgarran, where there was an old castle. The Dabharchú had sailed down the mountain on the Grange river, and reached Cashelgarran from the opposite direction.

Terence quickly concealed himself within the castle walls, and as the Dabharchú approached, he leapt out, drew his long sword and plunged it between the monster's eyes.

Now Lake Glenade is monster-free. Unless, of course, there was a little Dabharchú . . .

Above: The clear, deep waters of Ireland's lakes may still conceal the descendants of the Dabharchú – 'The Hound of the Deep' . . .

Right: The many lakes and inland waters of Connacht are well known for myths and legends of water monsters and enchantment.

St Patrick's Visit

Bay of Sligo

CONEY ISLAND, in the bay of Sligo, used to be known as Inis Coinin – the island of rabbits. When St Patrick visited the island, he hoped that one day it would be possible to build a church there.

He was invited to dine with one of the island families. His hostess, however, was distressed because she had no rabbit available to cook. But when the meal was served the problem had obviously been resolved, for the main dish appeared to be a delicious rabbit stew.

The saint blessed the food, and as he was about to eat it, a dog suddenly appeared. Immediately, a cat jumped up from St Patrick's plate and bounded out of the door.

The saint rose to his feet in anger. He said that because of what had happened, no church should ever be built on the island. Then, seeing the people's dismay, he added that every Sunday it would be possible for them to cross the seas to a church on the mainland.

So now Colney Islanders worship on Sundays without getting their feet wet – either crossing by boat to Rosses Point, or walking across the sands to Strandhill at low tide.

Right: Ben Bulben mountain, County Sligo.

The Sligo Duel

Bay of Sligo

EARLY IN the 19th century a ship foundered off the Sligo coast, near to the shore at Tireragh. A priest who saw the incident hurried to the house of a military man, Major Hillas.

The major boarded the ship and managed to save the vessel and many of the crew. Before his task was completed, however, the ship was boarded by another Sligo man, John Fenton.

Fenton threatened to throw Hillas into the sea, and with the help of his cousin, took charge of the wreck. He then challenged the major to a duel.

Pistols were used for duelling in Sligo, and the scene was set early one morning in Kilmacowen. Fenton used his cousin as 'second', and Major Hillas had for his 'second' another military man, who was, however, long retired and slightly lame.

Hillas announced that the laws of honour obliged him to defend himself, but that he bore no animosity to any man. Fenton was the first to fire. The major's own shot followed rapidly – but it was too late, and he was killed outright.

Court proceedings followed, but the judge seemed to think that Hillas had involved himself unnecessarily – and Fenton was acquitted.

Left: Powerful waves pound the cliffs at Inishmore on Aran Island.

Vera the Witch

County Sligo

THERE WAS once an old woman called Vera who possessed a 'fairy-life' – in other words, she was a witch. No one knew exactly how old she was, but she had been around for many hundreds of years.

She was often known as 'An Cailleach Bheara' – the Old Woman of Bheara, and her house was a cave on the edge of the Mountain of the Two Birds.

Now Vera had a magic cow, which, as well as bringing her wealth and prosperity, also gave the best milk in County Sligo. Many people were envious of this cow, but the wise ones knew Vera's powers, and would never attempt to steal it.

One man and his son were not so wise, however. They had coveted Vera's cow for a long time, and now decided to capture it. 'After all,' said the father, 'what harm could such an old woman do to us?'

Little did they know! But, like all malefactors, they had to find out for themselves. So, at dead of night, they crept into Vera's mountain garden and drove off the magic cow.

Vera heard the thieves as they passed her cave, and knew exactly what they were about. She seized her magic oak wand and, hurrying outside, touched the man and his son with it. Immediately they were turned to stone.

Right: Dramatic storm clouds gather over Ben Bulben.

Unfortunately, Vera slipped in the darkness and the wand also touched the cow. As the touch had been accidental, she had no way of bringing the animal back to life. Vera felt very sad, for it had been a most companionable cow – not to mention the wealth, prosperity and the best milk in Sligo!

Now the witch was poor and lonely, and furthermore, she felt her age. She sang:

'I am the Hag of Beare,
Fine petticoats I used to wear,
And now, gaunt with poverty,
I hunt for rags to cover me!'

The time had come to drown her 'fairy-life', and for this she needed very deep water. On top of the Mountain of the Two Birds is the Lake of the Two Geese. Vera asked the fairy wind to take her there.

The lake welcomed her, and in its depths she remains to this day. Occasionally, you may hear her song – although it sounds more like a gurgle!

Right: The gurgling waters of this waterfall may sound just like the song of Vera the Witch.

IRELAND – MYTHS AND LEGENDS

The Lovers

Diarmuid and Gráinne

Traditional

'A pity beyond all telling
is hid in the heart of love. . .
W.B. Yeats

TARA, IN County Meath, was where the early Irish kings lived and were crowned. In those days of long ago, there lived a beautiful princess called Gráinne. She was the daughter of the High King of Ireland, and her home was the great palace at Tara.

Finn MacCool, leader of the army of the Fianna, was growing old. He decided to take another wife, with whom he could end his days. He looked around, and asked the High King to permit him to marry his daughter, the Princess Gráinne.

The princess had little heart for the marriage to Finn, for she was young and lively. But her father was a man of wisdom whom she respected, and he gave his blessing to the union.

A great feast was held at the palace to celebrate the engagement, and all the Fianna were invited. Among them was Diarmuid O'Duibhne, one of the bravest and most handsome men of Finn's army. The young princess fell in love the moment she set eyes on him.

Gráinne whispered to Diarmuid of her love and, although he was greatly attracted to her, his loyalty to Finn made him reluctant to take advantage of the situation. Gráinne, recognizing how impossible it would be for Diarmuid to steal a wife from the leader of the Fianna, took the only course open to her. She put Diarmuid 'under geasa' to elope with her.

A *geasa* is a solemn oath which cannot be broken. The elopement was now assured. Gráinne poured drinks for everyone at the feast, with the exception of Diarmuid and his most trusted friends. A great drowsiness overcame those who had taken the drink – and soon they were asleep.

Diarmuid and Gráinne, with the help of his four friends, set out on a flight which was to last seven years. They fled to the banks of the Shannon, where Diarmuid carried the princess across the river. There he built a small hut, in which was their first 'leaba', or bed.

When Finn awoke and found Diarmuid and Gráinne were missing, his anger knew no bounds. He summoned the Clann Navin – the tracking men of the Fianna – and ordered them to find and capture the young couple.

Left: The ruins of Bective Abbey where the early Irish kings once lived, still stand in County Meath.
Far Left: Impressive views of Lough Tay, County Wicklow.

Above: Standing stones at Garrane, County Cork.

The Flight

Traditional

AT THE EDGE of the Shannon, the Clann Navin lost the tracks of their quarry. Finn, enraged by jealousy and hurt pride, told them that unless they took up the trail again speedily, they would all be hanged.

Diarmuid and Gráinne had a fine hiding place in a woodland hut, with barricaded doors facing seven different parts of the wood. But the Clann Navin, inspired by Finn's threat, tracked down the lovers and a sentry of the Fianna was placed on every side.

It happened that Diarmuid had a foster-father called Aongus na Brugh, who had learned magical powers from the wisest of the Druids. Aongus sensed that Diarmuid was in danger, and immediately flew to his aid.

He took Gráinne to safety from the hut, under his mantle of invisibility. Diarmuid, however, would not consent to leave in this fashion and so waited until one of the doors was unguarded.

Protecting himself with two spears, he then bounded through the door and raced to freedom, where Gráinne was anxiously waiting for him with Aongus. The lovers were overjoyed to be together again and thanked Aongus na Brugh for his help.

Before leaving the young couple, Aongus gave them instructions for their safety. He told them never to venture into a tree with only one trunk, nor a cave with only one opening,

Below: High cross at Kilfenora, County Clare.

Right: The sun sets at Kilmacduagh, near Gort, County Clare.

Far right: The imposing sight of Poulnabrone Dolmen, County Clare.

He warned them not to land on an island with only one channel leading to it, nor to stay to eat their food where they had cooked it – and never to eat in the same place where they had slept.

Finally, he cautioned them, 'Wherever you sleep tonight, do not sleep there tomorrow night.'

The lovers promised to follow his advice, and for seven years that was how they lived, always fleeing before the Fianna and the Clann Navin. But they were happy together, and

Diarmuid was a good hunter. After some years, however, they had four children to take with them, and flight became more difficult.

Aongus now encouraged Diarmuid to make peace with Finn, and offered to act as an intermediary between them. Finn's anger had not abated, but he had grown weary of the chase and so agreed to forgive Diarmuid and Gráinne.

The lovers and their children settled down happily to live in a place called Rath Ghráinne, in County Sligo.

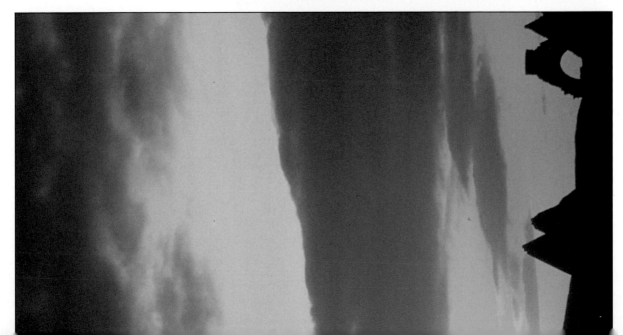

The Wild Boar

Traditional

ONE NIGHT, Diarmuid was awakened by the sound of dogs barking in the distance, and decided he should investigate. Gráinne sensed danger, and implored him not to go, but on this occasion he ignored her.

He came to Ben Bulben, where Finn and the Fianna had been hunting. Finn told him that the wild boar of Ben Bulben had already killed 50 of his men, and Diarmuid said he would take a hand at hunting the beast.

At that moment, the boar appeared on the peak of Ben Bulben. Diarmuid drew his sword and hit the animal on the back. The sword broke in two and Diarmuid was knocked off balance, but he quickly regained his footing and leapt on the boar's back.

The boar tore down the side of the mountain, trying to shake him off. But Diarmuid's grip was firm. Then it turned and rushed again to the top of Ben Bulben – whereupon Diarmuid quickly seized another sword and plunged it into the animal's skull. Before the boar died, it thrust its tusk into Diarmuid's side, fatally wounding him. As Diarmuid lay dying, he reminded Finn that he had the power to save his life.

'You know that you only have to carry the pure water of a spring well in your hands for me to drink,' he said weakly, 'and my wound will heal.'

Finn said there was no well on the mountain. But Diarmuid's friends in the Fianna pointed out

that there was a well only a few paces away. Finn placed his palms together and collected the water from the well.

Then, as he approached Diarmuid, he thought of the humiliation the younger man had caused

him, and let the water slip away through his fingers.

Diarmuid was becoming weaker, but he managed to persuade Finn to bring the healing water to him. Finn took the water between his palms again, but as he approached the dying man he

THE LOVERS

pretended to trip on a stone, and the water was lost. Then Finn, who alone could save Diarmuid, saw the cold eyes of the Fianna upon him.

This time he collected the water and brought it safely to the dying man. But he was too late.

Before he could drink, Diarmuid breathed his last breath on the side of the mountain.

Today, there is a special resting place on Ben Bulben, known as 'The Cave of Diarmuid and Gráinne'.

Above: Three Rocks, The Burren, County Clare – a landscape which evokes a past when High Kings ruled and giants did battle.

— 63 —

IRELAND – MYTHS AND LEGENDS

Legends of Munster & Leinster

The Lost Shadow

Munster

THERE WAS once a man in Munster named Brasil, who bought a small island from a Scottish chieftain. But the chieftain had to return to Scotland before the deal was completed.

Brasil travelled to Scotland after him, to get the papers for the island. He searched for the chieftain, until at last someone was able to direct him to his castle.

The chieftain welcomed Brasil, who explained that he had come to get the papers for his island. The chieftain took him into the library. 'I have them ready,' he said. 'But perhaps you would like to stay here with us.'

Brasil did not want to remain in the castle longer than he had to. So he thanked the chieftain, but said he must return to Munster.

'Then I shall have to keep your shadow,' said the chieftain.

Terrified, and determined not to lose his shadow, Brasil seized the papers and ran from the castle. But as he passed the library window, the sun cast his shadow into the room – and the chieftain put a book on it and held it there.

Today, if you meet anyone named Brasil, you will almost certainly find they have no shadow.

The Four-Leafed Shamrock

County Kerry

A SHOWMAN in Dingle had a cockerel that everyone thought was magic. The showman's trick was to have this cockerel walking down the street ahead of him, dragging a heavy wooden beam. At least, everyone thought that it was a beam of wood tied to the cockerel's leg, and which it dragged so effortlessly.

The crowd got ever bigger as the showman went from street to street, and the more people who followed him, the more money he made.

Then an old man came along the street carrying a bundle of rushes on his back. He thought everyone had gone mad to be following the showman like that. He could only see a cockerel dragging a piece of straw. He said as much to the showman, who asked him how much he wanted for his bundle of rushes. The old man named a good price, and the showman paid him.

Once the rushes had gone, the old man thought the cockerel was dragging a large wooden beam, and he, too, followed the crowd. Unbeknown to him, there was a four-leafed shamrock in his bundle – and that had made him see what others couldn't see!

Left: Poulnabrone Dolmens, County Clare, at sunset.
Right: Cashel Rock (4–12th century) the seat of the kings of Munster in County Tipperary.

The Magic Apron

County Cork

MANY YEARS ago, a girl who lived in County Cork used to go to Baltimore to sell buttermilk. She had the churn in a donkey cart, and would stand there selling the milk to anyone who wanted to buy it.

One day, a sailor asked for a quart of the milk. She gave it to him and he drank it, afterwards wiping his mouth on the corner of her apron.

As if in a trance, the girl followed him. She left the donkey, the cart and the milk churn and simply went wherever the sailor went.

Later that day her uncle, finding the donkey and the cart deserted, began to search for her. Eventually, he found her in a public house, standing close behind the sailor who had touched her apron.

She was a girl who never went into public houses, and her uncle knew some enchantment was afoot. Quickly, he cut the strings of her apron and then threw it on to the fire.

Immediately, the girl left the sailor and returned to her milk cart. There she continued to sell her buttermilk as if nothing had happened!

The Sacred Tree

County Waterford

THERE ARE many 'immortal trees' in Ireland. Some of them are very old indeed and some are self-renewing – or grow as the old tree dies. Sacred trees have been mentioned for centuries, and are generally attributed to the miracle of a saint.

One example is St Colman's sacred tree in the 'old parish' near Ardmore, County Waterford. Walking near his church one day, the saint put a small dry stick into the ground. He left it there and it took root, growing into a tree that can never be destroyed.

Few people would attempt to harm such a tree – aware of the punishment to follow. But a man from Ardmore once broke off some twigs from St Colman's sacred tree, and took them home to burn.

As he approached his house, it appeared to be on fire. He dropped the sticks and rushed to put out the flames. But when he reached home, there was no fire.

This happened a second, and then a third time. So he decided to ignore the illusion and carried the sticks all the way home. This time, on reaching his house, he found it had burnt to the ground.

Above: Lake scene, County Cork.

Left: The wild and rugged scenery of Conor Pass and Brandon Mountain on the Dingle Peninsular, County Kerry.

Right: Dunboy Castle, near Castletownbere, County Cork, commands impressive views over the lake.

Strange Stones

Floating Stones

County Cavan

IN IRELAND there are many stories of stone 'boats' and stones that float. St Mogue was born on an island in Templeport Lake in County Cavan, and the priest who baptized him crossed to the island on a large floating flagstone.

He returned to the mainland in the same manner, after which the stone was kept to ferry coffins to the island for burial. This practice continued until a courting couple decided to go sailing on the stone, and took it out on to the lake.

The stone, apparently insulted by such frivolous use, broke into three parts and the young couple were drowned.

St Barry once used a stone 'boat' to cross the river Shannon, and left it for the local people to use after he left. He told them that as long as they retained their innocence, the boat would continue to carry them across the river.

At some time they must have lost their innocence, because the stone boat sank. It was retrieved, however, and taken to Kilbarry Church in County Roscommon, where it can still be seen in the churchyard.

Returning Stones

County Kerry

SOME STONES are credited with very strange powers, and the 'returning' stones are perhaps the most extraordinary of all.

A fisherman of County Kerry once took a stone from the wall of a church. He attached it to a rope and put it into his boat, intending to use it as an anchor. When he had found a good place to fish, he put the stone overboard – but it came away from the rope to which he had attached it.

This surprised the fisherman, for his knots were usually very secure. Then, as he watched, the stone appeared to sink. That evening, while it was still light, he secured his boat and made his way home. As he passed the church, he was amazed to see that the stone was back in its place in the wall!

At Ardfert in County Kerry is a large stone slab beside a well. A soldier once used an ox cart to remove the stone, and when he got to Bulloch Hill the oxen refused to go any further – so he left the stone there overnight. The following morning, it was found to be back in its original place by the well.

Far left: Standing stones at Gerrane, County Cork.
Left: Stone circle at Castletown Bearhaven, County Cork.
Right: The portal tomb, Haroldstown, County Carlow, one of Ireland's many mysterious stone structures.

Legends of Finn MacCool

The Birth of Finn

Traditional

AT A PLACE that was called Cnucha – near where Dublin stands today – a great and bloody battle took place. It was between two Fianna chiefs: Cool Mac Trenmor of Leinster, who was also captain of all the Fianna, and Aed Mac Morna, chief of the Connacht Fianna.

One of Cool's warriors wounded Aed so severely in the eye that ever afterwards he went by the name of Goll – which means 'one-eyed'. His revenge was swift, for he took Cool Mac Trenmor's life, and the Fianna lost their captain.

News of Cool's death was brought to his young wife, Murna of the White Neck, who was about to bear his child. She knew that Cool's enemies would not allow any child of his to live, and so she fled with two of her most trusted women into the wildness of Slieve Bloom. There she bore a son whom she called Demna.

She gave the baby over to the safe keeping of her two women, bidding them to bring him up in the hidden glens until he was old enough to fight for his rightful place as Cool's son.

Left: Little Skellig, County Cork.

The Boyhood of Finn

Traditional

DEMNA'S CHILDHOOD was spent in Slieve Bloom, and the women trained him in the ways of the wild. By the time he was a youth, he could bring a bird out of the sky with a single cast of a sling stone, and run down the deer on his naked feet.

As he grew older, he wandered further from his bothie home. One day he came to the hall of a chieftain, in front of which some boys were playing hurley – an Irish stick and ball game.

He asked if he may join in, and soon he was able to play better than any of them, even taking the ball from their swiftest player. That night, the boys told the chieftain of the strange youth who had joined them and beaten them at hurley.

'We do not know his name,' said the leader among the boys, 'but he is tall and strong, and his hair is as bright as barley that has whitened in the sun.'

'Then there can only be one name for him,' said the chieftain, 'and that is Finn!' Finn means fair – and from that day forth, Finn he became.

Left: Dublin City at sunset, believed to be close to the site of a great battle.

The Salmon of Knowledge

Traditional

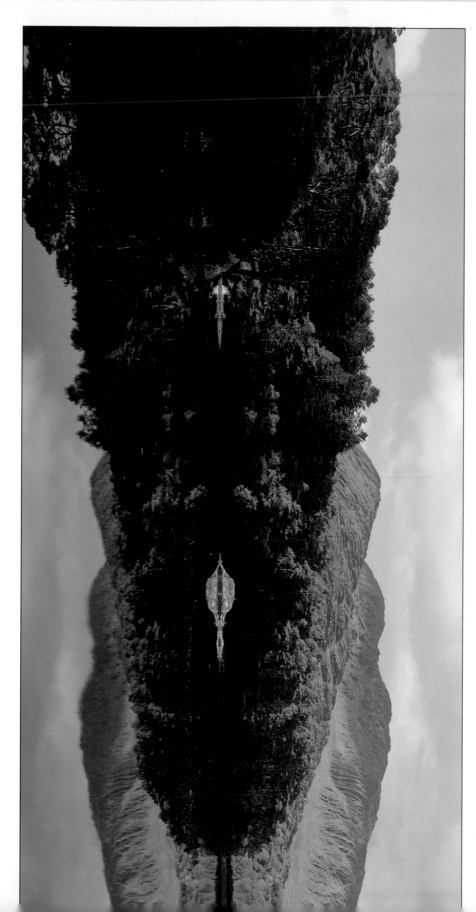

HE TIME had come for Finn to leave the hidden glens of Slieve Bloom, and his two foster mothers. Taking a spear and his sling, he set out on his travels.

He wandered the length and breadth of Erin, serving kings and chieftains and acquiring weapon-skills and warrior training. But before he was ready to take his father's place as leader of the

Fianna, he knew he must study poetry and ancient wisdom with the wise Druid, Finegas.

For seven years Finegas had lived beside the Boyne, trying to catch Fintan, the Salmon of

Knowledge. The salmon lived in a dark pool in the river, overhung by a hazel tree that dropped nuts of knowledge into the water. Finegas ate the nuts as they fell, and their power passed to him – but whoever ate Fintan would possess the wisdom of all the ages.

Strangely enough, as soon as Finn came to him as a pupil, Finegas caught the salmon quite easily.

He rather suspected that it had chosen its own time to be caught! He gave the fish to Finn to cook, warning him not to eat any of it himself.

'Bring the salmon to me as soon as it is ready,' Finegas told him, 'for I have been longing for the taste of it for seven years.' Then he repeated his warning, 'Eat nothing of it yourself – not even the smallest mouthful.'

He sat by his bothie door and waited for his pupil to bring the salmon. At last Finn came with it, hot and steaming on a maple wood dish. But as he set the fish down, Finegas looked into his face and saw that it was no longer the face of a boy.

'Have you eaten any of the salmon in spite of my words?' Finegas asked. Finn replied that he had not, but that as he turned the fish on the spit he scorched his thumb, and then sucked it to ease the pain. 'Was there any harm in that?' he asked anxiously.

'Take the rest of the salmon and eat it,' said Finegas, 'for in the hot juice on your thumb you have had all the knowledge in it. In you, and not in me, is the prophecy fulfilled. When you have eaten go from here, for I can teach you nothing more.'

Left: The breathtaking beauty of Lauragh, County Kerry.

Aillen of the Flaming Breath

Traditional

FINN KNEW that the time had come to claim his father's place, and he set out for Tara of the High Kings. There he swore faith to Cormac, the High King, and became one of his warriors.

It was Samhain, the time of the great autumn feast, and every Samhain at midnight for the past 20 years, Tara had been visited by a fiend. It came from the Fairy Hill close by and was called Aillen of the Flaming Breath, because it breathed fire on to thatch and timber and burned all the buildings of Tara.

No warrior could withstand the fiend, for it carried a silver harp and played the most beautiful music, putting all who heard it into an enchanted sleep. So every year, Tara had to be rebuilt.

Cormac offered gold and horses to any warrior who could defeat Aillen, and keep the thatch on Tara until the next day's dawn. Finn declared he would forgo the reward if, instead, Cormac swore to give him his rightful heritage – the leadership of the Fianna of Erin.

Cormac agreed, and Finn took up his sword, determined to succeed where so many had failed.

As he paced to and fro, waiting and watching, an older warrior came up to him, carrying a spear with its head in a leather hood.

Right: The sea mist rises at Galley Head, County Cork.

'Your father once saved my life,' the warrior told Finn. 'Take this spear, which was forged by Lein, the Smith of the Gods. Lay the blade to your forehead and the bloodlust in it will drive away all sleep.'

Finn took the spear and continued his pacing, watching and waiting. Then he heard it – harp music on the night air, soft and almost unbearably beautiful.

He felt the drowsiness of enchantment overcoming him, and held the cold steel blade of the spear to his forehead. Instantly, he was wide awake and confronting the hideous, wraith-like shape that bore down upon him, breathing a tongue of greenish fire as it came.

He threw the spear at the creature with all his might. Aillen of the Flaming Breath gave a terrible scream as the spear pierced the spot where its heart should have been. Then the fiend crumpled and died, and Finn cut off its head.

Cormac kept his word and set Finn, son of Cool, in his father's place as Captain of the Fianna.

Left: An aerial view of magnificent Slieve Elva, The Burren, County Clare.

Finn and the Fianna

Traditional

THE BROTHERHOOD of the Fianna consisted of warriors and hunters who protected Erin from invaders. They also kept down blood feuds between the five lesser kingdoms of Erin – Ulster, Munster, Connacht, Leinster and Mide.

While each kingdom had its own company of Fianna with its own captain, every Fianna member made his oath of loyalty to the Captain of the Fianna of Erin. An oath was also made to the High King of Erin himself, seated in his palace at Tara, with his right foot on the Stone of Destiny.

Finn MacCool, son of Cool Mac Trenmor, was now Captain of the Fianna. Cormac, the High King, gave him the Dun (hill-fort) of Almu,

in Kildare. Here Finn had a place to live, a great hall and a stronghold where he could gather his chief warriors about him.

The power of the Fianna was at its greatest while Finn was their captain. But to join was by no means easy – and many tried and failed.

Finn ruled that no man should become one of the proud brotherhood until he had passed a number of difficult tests. The first test of skill a young man had to undergo was to protect himself, with only a shield and a hazel rod, against nine men posted all around him with spears.

This was made even more difficult because he stood in a hole in the ground, unable to move his feet or legs. And if one of the spears so much as grazed his skin, he had failed the test.

Left: Romantic castles can still be found throughout Ireland and many of them remain private homes.

Next, his hair was plaited into braids, and he was hunted through the woods by warriors of the Fianna. If he was wounded, or his spear trembled in his hand, or a dry twig cracked beneath his feet – or even if a single strand of hair broke loose from its braiding, then he had failed and was not taken!

Finn himself was fearless, generous and just. He is said to have wept only twice in his lifetime; once for the death of Bran, his favourite hound, and once for the death of Osca, his grandson.

Today, the site of Finn's stronghold in Kildare is called the Hill of Allen. But all that can be seen now are traces of encircling turf banks, under the heather and brambles.

Left: The striking colours of the Wicklow Mountains, County Wicklow. Below: O'Brien's Tower overlooking the sea, County Clare.

Conan and the Enchantment

Traditional

CONAN MAOL was one member of the Fianna who was not very popular. He was fat, balding and fond of belittling other men's deeds. Finn only kept him because he had a good core of common sense, and his advice was often worth heeding.

There was, however, something very strange about Conan. Instead of human skin, he had black ram's fleece all over his back. This is how it happened.

One day, when Conan and others of the Fianna were out hunting, they came across a stately dun and entered in search of hospitality. They found themselves in a chieftain's hall, with white walls and silken drapes. There was no sign of a living creature, but in the centre of the hall was a table, set for a feast.

The fare was appetizing – venison, boar, sweet fruits and vats of rich, ruby wine. The Fianna were weary and hungry. They sat down at the table and helped themselves to food from the gold platters, and poured wine into the silver goblets.

They ate and drank with much merriment. But halfway through the meal, one of them sprang to his feet with a cry of warning.

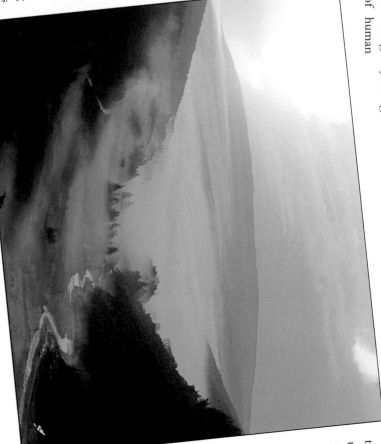

The others looked up, and saw that the hall was changing around them. The smooth walls were turning to rough wattle, and the fine thatched roof with its painted rafters was changing to smoke-blackened turf.

'Enchantment!' cried one of the warriors. They all sprang to their feet and made for the doorway, which was shrinking in size until it was little bigger than the opening to a fox's earth.

Conan Maol, however, was so busy eating that he failed to notice any of this until someone shouted to him. He then tried to rise, but found himself stuck fast to his chair. Terrified, he howled to the others for help, and two of them rushed back and seized him by the arms.

With a mighty effort, they managed to pull him free. But he left behind most of his tunic and breeches and all the skin on his back.

They managed to get him safely outside, but he was in such pain that the only thing they could do for him was to kill and flay a black ram, and cover his back with the skin. There it took root and grew, and was with him for the rest of his life.

Above and right: Mist and mood in the lovely Emerald Isle – undeniably a land of enchantment.

Index & Place Names